CASTE, CULTURE AND SOCIALISM

CASTE, CULTURE AND SOCIALISM

SWAMI VIVEKANANDA

GYAN

Published by

GYAN

Gyan Publishing House
5, Ansari Road
Daryaganj, New Delhi-110002
Phone: 011-47034999, 9811692060
E-mail: books@gyanbooks.com

Distribution Network
gyanbooks.com
India, USA, Canada, UK, Australia

ISBN: 978-93-6780-225-0 (PB)

First Published, 1947

2nd Impression 2024

Printed at: Gyan Press, Delhi.

CASTE, CULTURE AND SOCIALISM
Author: SWAMI VIVEKANANDA

CASTE, CULTURE AND SOCIALISM

SWAMI VIVEKANANDA

PREFACE

About twenty years ago a book, purporting to present the views of Swami Vivekananda on Socialism, was published; and on the fly-leaf was displayed in bold letters these words of Swamiji: "I am a Socialist." The book created some interest; but people steeped in the Vivekananda lore could easily see that the picture was over-coloured.

True, Swami Vivekananda had an intimate knowledge of such Western movements as Anarchism, Nihilism, Socialism and Communism from their literature as well as from personal contacts. He met Peter Kropotkin at the Paris International Exhibition (1900); and Plekhanoff's party was then very active in England. These movements were then in their infancy; and even their protagonists had no great hope for the causes they advocated. It was remarkable, therefore, for such an Orientalist as Swami Vivekananda to prophesy at that distant date that "Socialism of some form was coming on the boards" and that the Shudras as *Shudras* would be the future ruling caste. Besides, Vivekananda was never tired of drawing our attention to the source of our strength —the masses:

"Whether the leadership of society be in the hands of those who monopolise learning, or wield the power of riches or arms, the source of its power is always the subject masses. By so much, as the class in power severs itself from this source, by so much is it sure to become weak. But such is the strange irony of fate... that those from whom this power is directly or indirectly drawn... soon cease to be taken into account by the leading class."

People, reading the Vivekananda literature, are also impressed by his heartfelt sympathy for the poor and the downtrodden; and his dynamic appeal for serving them is irresistible:

"Feel for the miserable and look up for help —it *shall come*.... Go now this moment to the temple of Pârthasârathi, and before Him who was friend to the poor and lowly cowherds of Gokula, who never shrank to embrace the Pariah Guhaka—yea, down on your faces before Him and make a sacrifice, the sacrifice of a whole life for them, for whom He comes from time to time, whom He loves above all—the poor, the lowly, the oppressed!"

To Vivekananda's vision, the Shudras, the

Pariahs, were the proletariat of India, and the Indian Socialism was to be conceived in terms of their betterment. True, he could not condemn caste outright; for caste, fundamentally, was a glorious institution, and any future society must recognise its intrinsic worth. Nevertheless, Vivekananda had no love for the present-day hereditary caste-system which is a hindrance to progress. His wide sympathy could not be confined within its steel frame:

"Do you mean to say I am born to live and die one of those caste-ridden, superstitious, merciless, hypocritical, atheistic cowards that you find only amongst the educated Hindus?"

On the other hand, he was not much enamoured of a mere economic equality; he rather stood for a cultural and spiritual fraternity in which there would be not only economic Socialism and political freedom, but also moral and intellectual kinship. In short, he did not believe in levelling down, but rather in levelling up. His conception of the Golden Age was an age in which diversity of capacity and occupation would remain, but in which privilege would be totally unknown. This required a root-and-branch reform; but that reform could not come through a revolution based on force, it could be ushered in only through evolution based on culture and mutual esteem. Thus his motto seems to have been, "From caste to Socialism through culture." In the Golden Age, or the Socialistic Age of Swami Vivekananda's conception, all would be Brahmanas in the ideal sense of the term:

"In the beginning of the Satya Yuga (Golden Age) there was one caste, the Brahmanas; and then by difference of occupations they went on dividing themselves into different castes; and that is the only true and rational explanation that has been given. And in the coming Satya Yuga all the other castes will have to go back to the same condition. The solution of the caste problem in India, therefore, assumes this form—not to degrade the higher castes, not to crush out the Brahmana."

Evolution, however, was not to be confused with complacency. Vivekananda was up in arms against all social inequities. In his scheme of dynamic living certain things had no place. It was the bounden duty of the privileged classes to make a voluntary exit by rapidly handing over their culture to the masses. Delay would be dangerous : for that would mean an inevitable class-struggle, the foregone conclusion of which would be the supremacy of mere mass power: "There will be a great distribution of ordinary culture, but extraordinary geniuses will be less and less." For the priests he had hardly any soft word, because they could not avoid their responsibility for all the irrational developments in the Hindu Society in the form of regulations about food, marriage and untouchability etc. His quick, discerning mind could not fail to discover the heartless oddity of the situation. In fact, he called it lunacy:

"Was there ever a sillier thing before in the world than what I saw in Malabar country? The poor Pariah is not allowed to pass through the same street as the high-caste man, but if he changes his name to a hodge-podge English name, it is all right; or to a Mohammedan name, it is all right. What inference would you draw except that these Malabaris are all lunatics, their homes so many lunatic asylums, and that they are to be treated with derision by every race in India until they mend their manners and know better. Shame upon them that such wicked and diabolical customs are allowed! Their own children are allowed to die of starvation, but as soon as they take up some other religion they are well fed! ... The Mohammedan conquest of India came as a salvation to the downtrodden, to the poor. ...

That is why one-fifth of our people have become Mohammedans. . . . And one-fifth—one half—of your Madras people will become Christians if you do not take care."

Swami Vivekananda knew, however, that though he mentioned Malabar as a typical case, other parts of India were equally guilty. Indeed untouchability in some form or other was eating into the vitals of Hinduism itself:

"You Hindus have no religion; your God is in the kitchen, your Bible the cooking-pot. . . . People here have given up the Vedas, and all your philosophy is in the kitchen. The religion of India at present is 'Don't-touchism.'. . . The present Hinduism is a degradation."

Such a state of things was bad enough to upset a susceptible mind like Swami Vivekananda's. But his faith in his own country's ideal and goal rebelled against blind reform inspired by foreign propaganda. In fact, India was never in need of reformers and the Indians, on the whole, never stood against advance. India possessed enough idealism to supply the leaven for millions of years still to come. Furthermore, growth must be from within. Our society was caste-ridden to be sure ; but what society was not in some form or other? In some respects "Indian caste is better than the caste which prevails in Europe or America. I do not say, it is absolutely good." If, to remedy our defects, we were to learn something from the West, the basis of reconstruction was to be our own past, and we were not to proceed by denying its contribution. For "Where would be your learning and other things, if there were no caste? There would be nothing left for the Europeans to study if caste had never existed. The Mohammedans would have smashed everything to pieces." So the ideal society would be the one in which would be synthesised the Indian idea of spiritual integrity and the Western idea of social progress.

The greatest single factor that Swami Vivekananda brought to bear on these social problems was that spiritual vision of India which refused to study life in mere fragments, but viewed it as a dynamic whole comprising all states and stages, and leading humanity progressively to the highest goal. Indeed, India to him was a Divine Personality to be loved, and worshipped. His Socialism accordingly, was enunciated not in terms of rights and privileges to the component parts, but in those of service and duty to the whole. "All evils come," said he, "relying on differences. All good comes from faith in equality, in the underlying sameness and oneness of things." So his exhortation to his country was:'

"Oh India! ... Forget not that thy marriage, thy wealth, thy life are not for self-pleasure—are not for thy individual personal happiness; forget not that thou art born as a sacrifice to the *Mother's* altar; forget not that thy social order is but the reflex of the Infinite Universal Motherhood; forget not that the lower classes, the ignorant, the poor, the illiter ate, the cobbler, the sweeper, are thy flesh and blood, thy brothers. Thou brave one, be bold, take courage, be proud that thou art an Indian and proudly proclaim—'I am an Indian, every Indian is my brother.' Say—'The ignorant Indian, the poor and destitute Indian, is my brother.' Thou, too, clad with but a rag round thy loins proudly proclaim at the top of thy voice—'The Indian is my brother; the Indian is my life; India's gods and goddesses are my God; India's society is the cradle of my infancy, the pleasure-garden of my youth, the sacred heaven—the Varanasi (Benares)—of my old age.' Say brother—'The soul of India is my highest heaven, the good of India is my good,' and repeat and pray day and night—'O Thou Lord of Gauri, O Thou Mother of the

Universe, vouchsafe manliness unto me! O Thou Mother of Strength, take away my weakness, take away my unmanliness, and Make me a Man!' "

This, then, in brief, is what Vivekananda wanted Hinduism and India to be. But his message is scattered all over the pages of his works, and is not so palpably clear to casual readers. We, therefore, present all the excerpts on this subject in a systematised form, believing that this intensive study in the modern context of social and political re-thinking will be highly beneficial.

CONTENTS

CASTE, CULTURE AND SOCIALISM

I

THE BACKGROUND

How many gushing springs and roaring cataracts, how many icy rivulets and ever-flowing streamlets, issuing from the eternal snow-capped peaks of the Himalayas, combine and flow together to form the gigantic river of the gods — the Ganges — and rush impetuously towards the ocean! So, what a variety of thoughts and ideas, how many currents of forces, issuing from innumerable saintly hearts, and from the brains of geniuses of various lands have already enveloped India, the Land of Karma, the arena for the display of higher human activities![1]

A veritable ethnological museum! Possibly, the half-ape skeleton of the recently discovered Sumatra link will be found on search here too. The Dolmens are not wanting. Flint implements can be dug out almost anywhere.... Then there are the more historical varieties— the Negrito-Kolarian, the Dravidian and the Aryan. To these have been added from time to time, dashes of nearly all the known races, and a great many yet unknown.... An ocean of humanity, composed of these race waves, seething, boiling, struggling, constantly changing form, rising to the surface, and spreading and swallowing little ones, again subsiding — this is the history of India.[2]

From the fusion of these different types and races our modern societies, manners and customs began to be evolved. New ideas sprang up and new sciences began to be cultivated. One class of men went on manufacturing articles of utility and comfort, either by manual or intellectual labour. A second class took upon themselves the charge of protecting them, and all proceeded to exchange these things. And it so happened that a band of fellows who were very clever undertook to take these things from one place to another, and on the plea of remuneration for this, appropriated the major portion of their profit as their due. One tilled the ground, a second guarded the produce from being robbed, a third took it to another place, and a fourth bought it. The cultivator got almost nothing, he who guarded the produce took away as much of it, as he could, by force; the merchant who brought it to the market took the lion's share; and the buyer had to pay out of all proportion for the things, and smarted under the burden! The protector came to be known as the king; he who took the commodities from one place to another was the merchant. These two did not produce anything— but still snatched away the best part of things, and made themselves fat by virtually reaping most of the fruits of the cultivators' toil and labour. The poor fellow who produced all these things had often to go without his meals and cry to God for help![3]

Now, with the march of events, all these matters grew more and more involved, knots upon knots multiplied; and out of this tangled network has evolved our modern complex society. But the marks of bygone character persist, and do not die out completely.[4]

The whole of the Asiatic civilisation was first evolved on the plains near large rivers and on fertile soils— on the banks of the Ganges, the Yangtse-Kiang and the Euphrates. The original foundation of all these civilisations is agriculture, and in all of them the Daivi (divine) nature predominates. Most of the European civilisation, on the other hand, originated either in hilly countries or on the sea-coasts— piracy and robbery form the basis of this civilisation; there the Asuri (non-divine) nature is predominant.[5]

The European civilisation may be likened to a piece of cloth, of which these are the materials; its loom is a vast temperate hilly country on the sea-shore; its cotton, a strong warlike mongrel race formed by the intermixture of various races; its warp is warfare in defence of one's self and one's religion. . . . Its woof is commerce. The means to its civilisation is the sword; its auxiliary— courage and strength; its aim— enjoyment here and hereafter.[6]

The loom of the fabric of the Aryan civilisation is a vast, warm, level country, interspersed with broad, navigable rivers. The cotton of this cloth is composed of highly civilised, semi-civilised and barbarian tribes, mostly Aryan. Its warp is Varnâshramâchâra,* and its woof, the conquest of strife and competition in nature.[7]

The object of the peoples of Europe is to exterminate all in order to live themselves. The aim of the Aryans is to raise all up to their own level, nay even to a higher level than themselves. The means of European civilisa-

* The old Indian institution of the four castes (Brahman, Kshatriya, Vaishya and Shudra) and four stages of life (student life, householder's life, hermit life and life of renunciation).

tion is the sword; of the Aryans, the division into different Varnas. This system of division into different Varnas is the stepping-stone to civilisation, making one rise higher and higher in proportion to one's learning and culture. In Europe, it is everywhere victory to the strong, and death to the weak. In the land of Bharata, every social rule is for the protection of the weak.[8]

* * *

The names Brahmana, Kshatriya, etc....represent the status of a community in itself continuously fluctuating, even when it has reached the summit; and all further endeavours are towards fixity of the type by non-marriage, by being forced to admit fresh groups, from lower castes or foreign lands, within its pale. Whatever caste has the power of the sword, becomes Kshatriya; whatever learning, Brahmana; whatever wealth, Vaishya. The groups that have reached the coveted goal, indeed, try to keep themselves aloof from the new-comers, by making subdivisions in the same caste; but the fact remains that they coalesce in the long run. This is going on before our own eyes, all over India.... We are, in spite of our various castes, and in spite of the modern custom of marriage restricted within the subdivisions of a caste (though this is not universal), a mixed race in every sense of the term.[9]

The institution of caste has always been very flexible, sometimes too flexible to ensure a healthy uprise of the races very low in the scale of culture. It put, theoretically at least, the whole of India under the guidance—not of wealth, nor the sword—but of intellect—intellect chastened and controlled by spirituality. The leading caste in India is the highest of the Aryans—the Brahmanas. Though apparently different from the social methods of other nations, on close inspection, the Aryan method of caste will not be found so very different except on two points:

The first is, in every other country the highest honour belongs to the Kshatriya—the man of the sword.... In India, the highest honour belongs to the man of peace—the Sharman, the Brahmana, the man of God.... The second point is, the difference of *unit*. The law of caste in every other country takes the individual man or woman as the sufficient unit. Wealth, power, intellect or beauty suffices for the individual to leave the status of birth and scramble up to anywhere he can.

Here, the unit is all the members of a caste community. Here too, one has every chance of rising from a low caste to a higher or the highest; only, in this birth-land of Altruism, one is compelled to take his whole caste along with him.... If you want to rise to a higher caste in India, you have to elevate all your caste first, and then there is nothing in your onward path to hold you back.[10]

So, what is the basis of the Indian's social order? It is the caste law. I am born for the caste; I live for the caste.... Born in the caste, the whole life must be lived according to caste regulation. In other words, in the present-day language, ... the Western man is born individualistic, while the Hindu is socialistic—entirely socialistic.... So, I have no voice in my marriage, nor my sister. It is the caste that determines all that. We are married sometimes as children. Why? Because the caste says, if they have to be married any way without their consent, it is better that they are married early. . . . You may say, "Oh, they lose a great deal of enjoyment—those exquisite emotions of a man falling in love with a woman, and a woman falling in love with a man. . . ." But the Hindu says, "We are socialistic. For the sake of one man's or one woman's exquisite pleasure, we don't want to load misery on hundreds of others."[11]

Our castes and our institutions have been necessary to protect us as a nation, and when this necessity for self-preservation will no more exist, they will die a natural death. But the older I grow, the better I seem to think of these time-honoured institutions of India. There was a time when I used to think that many of them were useless and worthless; but the older I grow, the more I seem to feel diffidence in cursing any one of them, for each one of them is the embodiment of the experience of centuries.

A child of but yesterday, destined to die the day after to-morrow, comes to me and asks me to change all my plans; and if I hear the advice of that baby and change all my surroundings according to his ideas, I myself should be a fool, and no one else. Much of the advice, that is coming to us from different countries, is similar to this. Tell these wiseacres: I will hear you when you have made a stable society yourselves. You cannot hold on to one idea for two days, you quarrel and fail; you are born like moths in the spring and die like them in five minutes. You come up like bubbles and burst like bubbles too. First form a stable society like ours. First make laws and institutions that remain undiminished in their power through scores of centuries. Then will be the time to talk on the subject with you; but till then, my friend, you are only a giddy child.[12]

They say, there should be no caste. Even those who are in caste say, it is not a very perfect institution. But they say, when you find us another and a better one, we will give it up. They say, what will you give us instead? Where is there no caste? In your nation (U. S. A.) you are struggling all the time to make a caste. As soon as a man gets a bag of dollars, he says, "I am one of the Four Hundred." We (in India) alone have succeeded in making a permanent caste. Other nations are struggling and do not succeed. We have superstitions and evils enough. Would taking the superstitions and evils from your (Western) country mend matters? It is owing to caste that three hundred millions of people can find a piece of bread to eat yet. It is an imperfect institution, no doubt. But if it had not been for caste, you would have had no Sanskrit books to study. This caste made walls, around which all sorts of invasions rolled and surged, but found it impossible to break through.

That necessity has not gone yet (March 25, 1896); so caste remains.[13]

* * *

The solution is not by bringing down the higher, but by raising the lower up to the level of the higher. And that is the line of work that is found in all our books, in spite of what you may hear from some people whose knowledge of their own Scriptures and whose capacity to understand the mighty plans of the ancients are only zero. . . . What is the plan? The ideal at one end is the Brahmana, and the ideal at the other end is the Chandâla; and the whole work is to raise the Chandala up to the Brahmana. Slowly and slowly you find more and more privileges granted to them. There are books where you read such fierce words as these: "If the Shudra hears the Veda, fill his ears with molten lead; and if he remembers a line, cut his tongue out."... Later on this tone is modified a little; as for instance, "Do not disturb the Shudras, but do not teach them higher things." Then gradually we find in other Smritis, especially in those that have full power now, that if the Shudras imitate the manners and customs of Brahmanas, they do well; they ought to be encouraged. Thus it is going on. . . . Coming to plain facts, we find that all the castes are to rise slowly and slowly; however, there are thousands of castes and some are even getting admission into Brâhmanahood, for what prevents any caste from declaring they are Brahmanas? Thus, caste with all its rigour, has been created in that manner. Let us suppose that there are castes here with ten thousand people in each. If these put their heads together and say, "We will call ourselves Brahmanas," nothing can stop them; I have seen it in my own life. Some castes become strong, and as soon as they all agree, who is to say nay? Because, whatever it was, each caste was exclusive of the other. It did not meddle with others' affairs; even the several divisions of one caste did not meddle with the other divisions; and those powerful epoch-makers, Shankaracharya and others, were the great caste-makers.[14]

I do not propose any levelling of castes. Caste is a very good thing. Caste is the plan we want to follow. What caste really is, not one in a million understands. There is no country in the world without caste. In India, from caste we reach to the point where there is no caste. Caste is based throughout on that principle. The plan in India is to make everybody Brahmana, the Brahmana being the ideal of humanity. If you read the history of India, you will find that attempts have always been made to raise the lower classes. Many are the classes that have been raised. Many more will follow till the whole will become Brahmana. That is the plan. We have only to raise them without bringing down anybody.[15]

The ideal man of our ancestors was the Brahmana. . . . In Europe, there is my Lord the Cardinal, who is struggling hard and spending thousands of pounds to prove the nobility of his ancestors; and he will not be satisfied unless he has traced his ancestry to some dreadful tyrant, who lived on a hill, and watched the people passing by, and whenever he had the opportunity, sprang out on them and robbed them. . . . In India, ...you are of the highest caste when you can trace your ancestry to a Rishi, and not otherwise. Our ideal is the Brahmana of spiritual culture and renunciation. By the Brahmana ideal what do I mean? I mean the ideal Brahmananess in which worldliness is altogether absent and true wisdom is abundantly present. That is the ideal of the Hindu race.[16]

The Brahmana caste and the Brâhmanya qualities are two distinct things. In India, one is held to be a Brahmana by one's caste; but in the West, one should be known as such by one's Brahmanya qualities. As there are three Gunas—Sattva, Rajas and Tamas—so there are Gunas which show a man to be a Brahmana, Kshatriya, Vaishya or a Shudra. The qualities of being a Brahmana or a Kshatriya are dying out from the country; but in the West they have now attained to Kshatriyahood, from which the next step is Brahmanahood, and many there are who have qualified themselves for that.[17]

With the prevalence of the Sâttvika essence, a man becomes inactive and rests always in a state of deep Dhyâna or contemplation; with the prevalence of the Rajas, he does bad as well as good works; and with the prevalence of the Tamas again, he becomes inactive and inert. . . . The Sattva prevailing, the man is inactive, he is calm to be sure; but that inactivity is the outcome of the centralisation of great powers. That calmness is the mother of tremendous energy. . . . That man of predominating Sattva is the Brahmana, the worshipped of all. Has he to go about from door to door, begging others to worship him? . . . And mark you, those things which you see in pusillanimous, effeminate folk who speak in a nasal tone chewing every syllable, whose voice is as thin as of one who has been starving for a week, who are like a tattered wet rag, who never protest or are moved even if kicked by anybody—those are the signs of the lowest Tamas, those are the signs of death—not of Sattva—all corruption and stench. . . . During these last thousand years, the whole country is filling the air with the name of the Lord, and is sending its prayer to Him; and the Lord is never lending His ears to them. And why should He? When even man never hears the cries of the fool, do you think God will?. . . See the irony of it! Jesus Christ, the God of the Europeans, has taught: Have no enemy, bless them that curse you; . . . stop all work and be ready for the next world. . . . And our Lord in the Gita is saying: Always work with great enthusiasm, destroy your enemies and enjoy the world. But, after all, it turned out to be exactly the reverse of what Christ or Krishna implied. . . . who are following the teachings of the Gita?—The Europeans! And who are acting according to the will of Jesus Christ?—The descendants of Sri Krishna![18]

Now you understand whether there are Brahmanas in the West or not. You have Brahmanas here (in India) also; but they are bringing the country down to the verge of ruin by their awful tyranny, and consequently what they have naturally is vanishing away by degrees.[19]

My disciples are all Brahmanas! ... The son of a Brahmana is not necessarily always a Brahmana; though there is every possibility of his being one, he may not become so. Did you not hear that the nephew of Aghore Chakravarty of Baghbazar became a sweeper, and actually used to do all the menial services of his adopted caste? Was he not the son of a Brahmana?[20]

As there are Sattva, Rajas and Tamas—one or other of these Gunas more or less—in every man, so the qualities which make a Brahmana, Kshatriya, Vaishya, or a Shudra are inherent in every man, more or less. But at times one or other of these qualities predominates in him in varying degrees and is manifested accordingly. Take a man in his different pursuits, for example; when he is engaged in serving another for pay, he is in Shudrahood; when he is busy transacting some piece of business for profit, on his own account, he is a Vaishya; when he fights to right wrongs, then the qualities of a Kshatriya come out in him; and when he meditates on God, or passes his time in conversation about Him, then he is a Brahmana. Naturally, it is quite possible for one to be changed from one caste into another. Otherwise, how did Vishvâmitra become a Brahmana, and Parashurâma a Kshatriya?[21]

We find clear proofs about caste being based on qualification both in the Bhishma-Parva of the Mahabharata and in the stories there of the Ajagara and of Umâ and Maheshvara.[22]

Every individual is a centre for the manifestation of a certain force. This force has been stored up as the resultant of our previous works; and each one of us is born with this force at his back.[23]

This is the great truth which the Lord Sri Krishna, the Revealer of the Gita, has tried therein to explain; and upon this great truth is established the Varnashrama system and the doctrine of Svadharma, etc. of the Hindu religion.[24]

It is only the Vedic religion which considers ways and means and lays down rules for the fourfold attainment of man, comprising Dharma, Artha (wealth), Kâma (enjoyment) and Moksha (salvation)......The right and correct means is that of the Vedas—the Jâti Dharma, that is the Dharma enjoined according to different castes—the Svadharma, that is one's own Dharma, or set of duties prescribed for man according to his capacity and position—which is the very basis of Vedic religion and Vedic society... This Jâti Dharma, this Svadharma, is the path of welfare of all societies in every land, the ladder to ultimate freedom. With the decay of this Jâti Dharma, the Svadharma, has come the downfall of our land. But the Jâti Dharma or Svadharma, as commonly understood at present by the higher castes, is rather a new evil, which has to be guarded against. They think; they know everything of Jâti Dharma, but really they know nothing of it. Regarding their own village custom as the eternal custom laid down by the Vedas, appropriating to themselves all privileges, they are going to their doom! I am not talking of caste as determined by qualitative distinction, but of the hereditary caste system. I admit that the qualitative caste system is the primary one; but the pity is, qualities yield to birth in two or three generations. Thus the vital point of our national life has been touched; otherwise, why should we sink to this degraded state? Read in the Gita, "I should then be the cause of the admixture of races, and I should ruin these beings." How came this terrible Varnasamkara—this confounding mixture of all castes and disappearance of all qualitative distinctions? Why has the white complexion of our forefathers now become black? Why did the Sattvaguna give place to the prevailing Tamas with a sprinkling, as it were, of Rajas in it? That is a long story to tell, and I reserve my answer for some future occasion. For the present, try to understand this that, if the Jâti Dharma be rightly and truly preserved, the nation shall never fall. If this is true, then what was it that brought our downfall? That we have fallen is the sure sign that the basis of the Jâti Dharma has been tampered with. Therefore, what you call the Jâti Dharma is quite contrary to what we have in fact. First, read your own Shâstras through and through, and you will easily see that what the Shâstras define as caste-Dharma, has disappeared almost everywhere from the land. Now, try to bring back the true Jâti Dharma and then it will be a real and sure boon to the country.[25]

II

IN TUNE WITH THE PAST

The modern inhabitants of the land of Bharata are not the glory of the ancient Aryans. But as fire remains intact under cover of ashes, so the ancestral fire still remains latent in these modern Indians. Through the grace of the Almighty Power, it is sure to manifest itself in time. What will accrue when the ancestral fire manifests itself?

Are the laws of Manu going to be rehabilitated as of yore? Or is the discrimination of food, prescribed and forbidden, varying in accordance with geographical dimensions, as it is at the present day, alone going to have its all-powerful domination over the length and breadth of the country? Is the caste-system to remain, and is it going to depend eternally upon the birthright of a man, or is it going to be determined by his qualification? And again, in that caste-system—is the discrimination of food, its touchableness and untouchableness, dependent on the purity or impurity of the man who touches it, to be observed as it is in Bengal, or will it assume a form more strict as it does in Madras? Or, as in the Punjab, will all such restrictions be obliterated? Are the marriages of different Varnas to take place from the upper to the lower Varna in the successive order, as in Manu's days, and as it is still in vogue in Nepal? Or, as in Bengal and other places, are they to be kept restricted to a very limited number of individuals constituting one of the several communities of a certain class of the Varna? To give a conclusive answer to all these questions is extremely difficult. They become the more difficult of solution, considering the difference in the customs prevailing in different parts of the country—nay, as we find even in the same part of the country, such a wide divergence of customs among different castes and families.[1]

* * *

All healthy social changes are the manifestations of the spiritual forces working within and if these are strong and well adjusted, society will arrange itself accordingly. Each individual has to work out his own solution; there is no other way, and so also with nations. Again, the great institutions of every nation are the conditions of its very existence and cannot be transformed by the mould of any other race. Until higher institutions have been evolved, any attempt to break the old ones will be disastrous. Growth is always gradual.[2]

Every improvement in India requires first of all an unheaval in religion. Before flooding India with socialistic or political ideas, first deluge the land with spiritual ideas.[3]

Everything goes to show that Socialism or some form of rule by the people, call it what you will, is coming on the boards. The people will certainly want the satisfaction of their material needs, less work, no oppression, no war, more food. What guarantee have we that this, or any civilisation, will last, unless it is based on religion, on the goodness of man? Depend on it, religion goes to the root of the matter. If it is right, all is right.[4]

Therefore, our solution of the caste question is not degrading those who are already high up, is not running amuck through food and drink, is not jumping out of our own limits in order to have more enjoyment, but it comes by every one of us fulfilling the dictates of our Vedantic religion, by our attaining spirituality, and by our becoming the ideal Brâhmana. There is a law laid down on each one of you in this land by our ancestors, whether you are Aryans, or non-Aryans, Rishis or Brahmanas, or the very lowest outcastes. The command is the same to you all, that you must make progress without stopping, and that, from the highest man to the lowest Pariah, every one in this country has to try and become the ideal Brahmana.. Such is our ideal of caste, as meant for raising all humanity slowly and gently towards the realisation of the great ideal of the spiritual man, who is non-resisting, calm, steady, worshipful, pure and meditative. In that ideal there is God...

Have you not heard how it is declared that he, the Brahmana, is not amenable to law, that he has no law, that he is not governed by kings, and that his body cannot be hurt? That is perfectly true. Do not understand it in the light thrown upon it by interested and ignorant fools, but understand it in the light of the true and original Vedantic conception. If the Brahmana is he who has killed all selfishness and who lives and works to acquire and propagate wisdom and the power of love —if a country is altogether inhabited by such Brahmanas, by men and women who are spiritual and moral and good, is it strange to think of that country as being above and beyond all law? What police, what military are necessary to govern them?... They are good and noble, and they are the men of God; these are our ideal Brahmanas; and we read that in the Satya Yuga there was only one caste, and that was the Brahmana. We read in the Mahabharata that the whole world was in the beginning peopled with Brahmanas, and that as they began to degenerate they became divided into different castes, and that when the cycle turns round they will go back to that Brahmanical origin. This cycle is turning round now; and I draw your attention to this fact.[5]

From the very date that he (Sri Ramakrishna) was born, has sprung the Satya-Yuga (Golden Age). Henceforth there is an end to all sorts of distinctions, and every one down to the Chandala will be sharer in the Divine Love. The distinction between man and woman, between the rich and poor, the literate and illiterate, Brahmanas and Chandalas—he lived to root out all. And he was the harbinger of Peace—the separation between Hindus and Mohammedans, between Hindus and Christians, all are now things of the past.

That fight about distinctions that there was, belonged to another era. In this Satya Yuga the tidal wave of Sri Ramakrishna's Love has unified all.[6]

I believe that the Satya Yuga will come when there will be one caste, one Veda, and peace and harmony. This idea of Satya Yuga is what would revivify India. Believe it...... Up boys, and put yourselves to the task! Old Hinduism for ever! Up, up, my boys, we are sure to win![7]

* * *

By degrees all the people of the land have to be lifted to the position of Brahmanas...... Each Hindu, I say, is a brother to every other, and it is we who have degraded them by our outcry, "Don't touch," "Don't touch!" And so the whole country has been plunged to the utmost depths of meanness, cowardice and ignorance. Those men have to be uplifted; words of hope and faith have to be proclaimed to them. We have to tell them, "You are also men like us and you have all the rights that we have." Do you understand?[8]

India is to be raised, the poor are to be fed, education is to be spread, and the evil of priestcraft is to be removed. No priestcraft, no social tyranny!... Our young fools make meetings to get more power from the English. They only laugh. None deserves liberty who is not ready to give liberty. Suppose the English give over to you all the power. Why, the powers that be then, will hold the people down, and let them not have it. Slaves want power to make slaves.

Now, this is to be brought about slowly and by only insisting on our religion, and giving liberty to society. Root up priestcraft from the old religion and you get the best religion in the world. Do you understand me? Can you make a European society with India's religion? I believe it is possible and must be.[9]

From the time of the Upanishads down to the present day, nearly all our great Teachers have wanted to break through the barriers of caste, i.e., caste in its degenerate state, not the original system. What little good you see in the present caste clings to it from the original caste, which was the most glorious social institution. Buddha tried to re-establish caste in its original form. At every period of India's awakening, there have always been great efforts made to break down caste. But it must always be *we* (Indians) who build up a new

India as an effect and continuation of her past, assimilating helpful foreign ideas wherever they may be found. Never can it be *they* (the foreigners); growth must proceed from within.[10]

Oh, we are awfully poor, and our masses are very ignorant about secular things. Our masses are very good because poverty here is not a crime. Our masses are not violent.... We have to give them secular education. We have to follow the plan laid down by our ancestors, that is, to bring all the ideals slowly down among the masses. Raise them slowly up, raise them to equality. Impart even secular knowledge through religion.... All the social upheavalists, at least the leaders of them, are trying to find that all their communistic or equalising theories must have a spiritual basis; and that spiritual basis is in the Vedanta only. I have been told by several leaders who used to attend my lectures, that they required the Vedanta as the basis of the new order of things.[11]

Aye, if there is anything in the Gita that I like, it is these two verses, coming out strong as the very gist, the very essence, of Krishna's teaching—"He who sees the Supreme Lord dwelling alike in all beings, the Imperishable in things that perish, he sees indeed. For seeing the Lord as the same, everywhere present, he does not destroy the Self by the Self; and thus he goes to the highest goal."... This wonderful idea of the sameness and omnipresence of the Supreme Soul has to be preached for the amelioration and elevation of the human race, here as elsewhere. Wherever there is evil and wherever there is ignorance and want of knowledge, I have found out by experience that all evil comes, as our Scriptures say, relying upon differences, and that all good comes from faith in equality, in the underlying sameness and oneness of things. This is the great Vedantic ideal.[12]

On the other hand, our experience is that if ever the followers of any religion approached to this equality in an appreciable degree in the plane of practical workaday life—it may be quite unconscious generally of the deeper meaning and the underlying principle of such conduct, which the Hindus, as a rule, so clearly perceive—it is those of Islam and Islam alone.... For our own motherland a junction of the two great systems, Hinduism and Islam —Vedanta brain and Islam body—is the only hope.[13]

Liberty of thought and action is the only

condition of life, of growth and well-being. Where it does not exist, the man, the race, the nation must go down. Caste or no caste, creed or no creed, any man, or class, or caste, or nation, or institution which bars the power of free thought and action of an individual—even so long as that power does not injure others—is devilish and must go down... Keep the motto before you—"Elevation of the masses without injuring the religion." Can you raise them? Can you give them back their lost individuality without making them lose their innate spiritual nature? Can you become an occidental of occidentals in your spirit of equality, freedom, work and energy, and at the same time a Hindu to the very backbone in religious culture and instincts? ... Onward for ever! Sympathy for the poor, the downtrodden, even unto death—this is our motto. Onward brave lads![14]

The Hindu must not give up his religion, but must keep religion within its proper limits and give freedom to society to grow. All the reformers in India made the serious mistake of holding religion accountable for all the horrors of priestcraft and degeneration, and went forth to pull down the indestructible structure; and what was the result?

Failure! Beginning from Buddha down to Ram Mohan Roy, everyone made the mistake of holding caste to be a religious institution, and tried to pull down religion and caste all together, and failed. But in spite of all the ravings of the priests, caste is simply a crystallised social institution, which after doing its service is now filling the atmosphere of India with its stench; and it can only be removed by giving back to the people their lost social individuality Every man born here (in U.S.A.) knows that he is a man. Every man born in India knows that he is a slave of society. Now, freedom is the only condition of growth; take that off, the result is degeneration. With the introduction of modern competition, see how caste is disappearing fast! No religion is now necessary to kill it. The Brahmana shopkeeper, shoemaker, and wine-distiller are common in Northern India. And why? Because of competition. No man is prohibited from doing anything he pleases for his livelihood under the present Government; and the result is neck and neck competition. And thus thousands are seeking and finding the highest level they were born for, instead of vegetating at the bottom.[15]

The English Government has been the instrument, brought over here by the Lord, to break your crystallised civilisation.[16]

* * *

There are two sorts of truth we find in our Shastras, one that is based upon the eternal nature of man—the one that deals with the eternal relation of God, soul and nature, the other, with local circumstances, environments of the time, social institutions of the period, and so forth. The first class of truths is chiefly embodied in our Vedas, our Scriptures; the second in the Smritis, the Puranas, etc. We must remember that for all periods the Vedas are the final goal and authority, and if the Puranas differ in any respect from the Vedas, that part of the Puranas is to be rejected without mercy.... Now, this is one of the most glorious doctrines that you have, that eternal truths, being based upon the nature of man, will never change so long as man lives; they are for all times, omnipresent, universal virtues. But the Smritis speak generally of local circumstances, of duties arising from different environments, and they change in the course of time. This you have always to remember, that because a little social custom is going to be changed you are not going to lose your religion, not at all. Remember these customs have already been changed.... As time rolls on, more and more of the Smritis will go, sages will come, and they will change and direct society into better channels, into duties and into paths according to the necessity of the age, and without which it is impossible that society can live.... I want the intensity of the fanatic plus the extensity of the materialist. Deep as the ocean, broad as the infinite skies, that is the sort of heart we want. Let us be as progressive as any nation that ever existed and at the same time as faithful and conservative towards our traditions as Hindus alone know how to be.[17]

Sudden changes cannot be, and Shankaracharya new it. So did Ramanuja. The only way left to them was slowly to bring up to the highest ideal, the existing religion. If they had sought to apply the other method, they would have been hypocrites, for the very fundamental doctrine of their religion is evolution.[18]

Where do you find the Indian Society standing still? It is always on the move.... Caste is continually changing, rituals are continually changing, so are forms. It is the substance, the principle, that does not change. It is in the Vedas that we have to study our religion. With the exception of the Vedas every book must change.... For instance, one Smriti is powerful for one age, another for another age.... Caste should not go; but should only be readjusted accordingly. Within the old structure is to be found life enough for the rebuilding of two hundred thousand new ones. It is sheer nonsense to desire the abolition of caste. The new method is—evolution of the old.[19]

Do you read the history of India? Who was Ramanuja? Who was Shankara? Who was Nanak? Who was Chaitanya? Who was Kabir? Who was Dadu? Who were all these great preachers, one following the other, a galaxy of stars of the first magnitude? Did not Ramanuja feel for the lower classes? Did he not try all his life to admit even the Pariah to his community? Did he not try to admit even Mohammedans to his own fold? Did not Nanak confer with Hindus and Mohammedans, and try to bring about a new state of things? They all tried and their work is still going on. The difference is this. They had not the fanfaronade of the reformers of to-day; they had no curses in their lips as modern reformers have, their lips pronounced only blessings. They never condemned. They said to the people that the race must grow. They looked back and they said, "O Hindus, what you have done is good, but my brothers, let us do better."...We must grow according to our nature. Vain is it to attempt the lines of action that foreign societies have engrafted upon us; it is impossible.[20]

* * *

There are two great obstacles on our path in India, the Scylla of old orthodoxy and the Charybdis of modern European civilisation.[21]

As Western ideas of organisation and external civilisation are penetrating and pouring into our country, whether we will have them or not, so Indian spirituality and philosophy are deluging the land of the West. None can resist it, and no more can we resist some sort of material civilisation from the West. A little of it, perhaps, is good for us, and a little spiritualisation is good for the West; thus the balance will be preserved. It is not that we ought to learn everything from the West, or that they have to learn everything from us; but each will have to supply and hand down to future generations what it has, for the future accomplishment of the dream of ages, the harmony of nations, an ideal world.[22]

As regards spirituality, the Americans are far inferior to us; but their society is far superior to ours. We will teach them our spirituality and assimilate what is best in their society.[23]

We have not given any freedom to the expansion of social matters, and ours is a cramped society.... In India, we have to take off the shackles from society; in Europe, the chains must be taken from the feet of spiritual progress.[24]

In Western countries there is no botheration of (hereditary) caste. Those on whom Fortune smiles for their industry and exertion, are alone regarded as leaders of the country and the controllers of its destiny. Whereas in your country (India) you are simply vaunting of your superiority in caste, till at last you cannot even get a morsel of food! You have not the capacity to manufacture a needle and you dare to criticise the English—fools![25]

To become broad, to go out, to amalgamate, to universalise, is the end of our aims. And all the time we have been making ourselves smaller and smaller, and dissociating ourselves, contrary to the plans laid down in our

Scriptures.... What can you expect of a race which for hundreds of years has been busy in discussing such momentous problems as whether we should drink a glass of water with the right hand or the left? What more degradation can there be than that the greatest minds of a country have been discussing about the kitchen for several hundreds of years, discussing whether I may touch you or you touch me, and what is the penance for this touching![26]

We have to find our way between the Scylla of old superstitious orthodoxy and the Charybdis of materialism—of Europeanism, of soullessness, of the so-called reform—which has penetrated to the foundation of Western progress. These two have to be taken care of. In the first place, we cannot become Westerners; therefore imitating the Westerners is useless.... In the second place, it is impossible.... Do you think it is possible for you to throw off the culture of shining scores of centuries? It cannot be. We must also remember that in every little village-god, and every little superstitious custom, is that which we are accustomed to call our religious faith. But local customs are infinite and contradictory; which are we to obey, and which not to obey? The

Brahmana in Southern India, for instance, would shrink in horror at the sight of another Brahmana eating meat; a Brahmana in the North thinks it a most glorious and holy thing to do—he kills goats by the hundred in sacrifice. If you put forward your custom, they are ready with theirs.[27]

The restrictions of caste are here (in Ceylon) much less than in India, the Buddhists have a few in marriage affairs, but none in matters of food, in which respect the Hindus observe some restrictions.... All the Hindu castes have mixed together and formed a single Hindu caste, in which like the Punjabi Jats, one can marry a girl of any caste—even a European girl at that. The son goes into a temple, puts the sacred trilinear marks on the forehead, utters "Shiva, Shiva," and becomes a Hindu. The husband may be a Hindu, while the wife is a Christian. The Christian rubs some sacred ash on the forehead, utters "Namah Parvatipataye" (Salutation to Shiva), and he straightway becomes a Hindu.[28]

Various are the customs all over India; but they are local. The greatest mistake made is, the ignorant people always think that this local custom is the essence of our religion.[29]

* * *

Though our castes and our institutions are apparently linked with our religion, they are not so.[30]

The caste-system is opposed to the religion of the Vedanta. Caste is a social custom, and all our great preachers have tried to break it down. From Buddhism downwards, every sect has preached against caste, and every time it has only riveted the chains. Caste is simply the outgrowth of the political institutions of India; it is a hereditary trade guild. Trade competition with Europe has broken caste more than any teaching.[31]

In religion there is no caste; caste is simply a social custom.[32]

Let distinctions of sex, caste, wealth, learning and the whole host of them, which are so many gateways to hell, be confined to the world alone.... Those who even in a chapel, would think this is a public woman, that man is of a low caste, a third is poor, and yet another belongs to the masses—the less be the number of such people, the better. Will they who look to the caste, sex or profession of Bhaktas appreciate our Lord?[33]

Any man, whether he be a Shudra or a Chandala can expound philosophy even to a Brahmana. The Truth can be learnt from the lowest individual, no matter to what caste or creed he belongs.[34]

Most of the Upanishads were written by Kshatriyas.... Most of our great teachers throughout India have been Kshatriyas, and were always universal in their teachings;.... Rama, Krishna, and Buddha—worshipped as incarnations of God—were Kshatriyas.[35]

The religion of the Hindus is divided into two parts, the ceremonial and the spiritual; the spiritual portion is specially studied by the monks. In that there is no caste. A man from the highest caste and a man from the lowest may become a monk in India, and the two castes become equal.[36]

One must admit that law, government, politics are phases, not final in any way. There is a goal beyond them where law is not needed. And, by the way, the very word Sannyasin means the divine outlaw, one might say, divine Nihilist, but that miscomprehension pursues those that use such a word.[37]

In the Buddha Incarnation the Lord says that the root of the Adhibhautika misery, or misery arising from other terrestrial beings, is the formation of classes (Jati); in other words, every form of class-distinction, whether based on birth or acquirements or wealth is at the bottom of this misery. In the Atman there is no distinction of sex or Varna or Ashrama or anything of the kind; and as mud cannot be washed away by mud, it is likewise impossible to bring about oneness by means of separative ideas.[38]

As for myself, I have no partiality for any party in this caste question, because I know it is a social law and is based on Diversity of Guna and Karma. It also means grave harm if one bent on going beyond Guna and Karma cherishes in mind any caste distinctions.[39]

The conviction is daily gaining on my mind that the idea of the caste is the greatest dividing factor and the root of Maya—all caste either on the principle of birth or of merit is bondage. Some friends advise, "True; lay all that at heart; but outside, in the world of relative experience, distinctions like caste must needs be maintained.... The idea of oneness at heart (with a craven impotence of effort, that is to say), and outside, the hell-dance of demons—oppression and persecution—aye, the dealer of death to the poor, but if the Pariah be wealthy enough, "Oh, he is the protector of religion!"

Over and above, I come to see from my studies that the disciplines of religion are not for the Shudra; if he exercises any discrimination about food or about going out to foreign lands, it is all useless in his case, only so much labour lost. I am a Shudra, a Mlechchha, so I have nothing to do with all that botheration. To me what would Mlechchha's food matter or Pariah's? It is in the books written by the priests that madnesses like that of caste are to be found, and not in books revealed from God. Let the priests enjoy the fruits of their ancestors' achievement, while I follow the word of God; for my good lies there.[40]

The Lord has shown me that religion is not at fault, but it is the Pharisees and Sadducees in Hinduism, hypocrites, who invent all sorts of engines of tyranny in the shape of doctrines of Pâramârthika and Vyâvahârika. . . . No religion on earth preaches the dignity of humanity in such a lofty strain as Hinduism, and no religion on earth treads upon the necks of the poor and the low in such a fashion as Hinduism.[41]

I read in the organ of the social reformers that I am called a Shudra, and am challenged as to what right a Shudra has to become a Sannyasin. To which I reply—I trace my descent to one at whose feet every Brahmana lays flowers when he utters the words —यमाय

धर्मराजाय चित्रगुप्ताय वै नमः— and whose descendants are the purest of Kshatriyas.... This is only by the way. I just refer to this, but I am not at all hurt if they call me a Shudra. It will be a little reparation for the tyranny of my ancestors over the poor. If I am a Pariah, I will be all the more glad, for I am the disciple of a man, who—the Brahmana of Brahmanas—wanted to cleanse the house of a Pariah. Of course the Pariah would not allow him....And this man woke up in the dead of night, entered surreptitiously, the house of this Pariah, cleansed his latrines and with his long hair wiped the place.... That hero's life I shall try to imitate.... One ounce of practice is worth twenty thousand tons of big talk.[42]

III

PRIEST AND PRIVILEGE

Priests believe that there is a God, but that this God can be approached and known only through them. People can enter the Holy of the Holies only with the permission of the priests. You must pay them, worship them, place everything in their hands. Throughout the history of the world, the priestly tendency has cropped up again and again—this tremendous thirst for power, this tiger-like thirst, seems a part of human nature. The priests dominate you, lay down a thousand rules for you. They describe simple truths in roundabout ways. They tell you stories to support their own superior position....

The priests in India, the Brahmanas, possessed great intellectual and psychic powers. It was they who began the spiritual development of India, and they accomplished wonderful things. But the time came when the free spirit of development that had at first actuated the Brahmanas, disappeared. They began to arrogate powers and privileges to themselves.

If a Brahmana killed a man, he would not be punished. The Brahmana, by his very birth, is the Lord of the Universe! Even the most wicked Brahmana must be worshipped![1]

In India, priesthood, like every other business in a social life, is a hereditary profession. A priest's son will become a priest, just as a carpenter's son will become a carpenter, or blacksmith's son a blacksmith.[2]

The orthodox Hindus are very exclusive, living entirely within their own horizon of thought and feeling. Their lives are laid down in our old books in every little detail, and the least detail is grasped with almost adamantine firmness by them.... The higher the caste, the greater the restrictions. The lowest caste people can eat and drink anything they like, but as men rise in the social scale, more and more restrictions come, and when they reach the highest caste, the Brahmana, the hereditary priesthood of India, their lives ... are very much circumscribed.[3]

Naturally, a group having raised itself would try to preserve the privileges to itself. Hence, whenever it was possible to get the help of the king, the higher castes, especially the Brahmanas, have tried to put down similar aspirations in lower castes, by the sword if practicable.

But the question is, did they succeed? Look closely into your Puranas and Upa-puranas, look especially into the local Khandas of the big Puranas, look round and see what is happening before your eyes; and you will find the answer.[4]

* * *

The foundation of the priestly power rests on intellectual strength, and not on the physical strength of arms. Therefore, with a supremacy of the priestly power, there is a great prevalence of intellectual and literary culture.... The priest knows the gods and communicates with them; he is, therefore, worshipped as a god. Leaving behind the thoughts of the world, he has no longer to devote himself to the earning of his bread by the sweat of his brow.... The first offshoot of universal welfare and good is nursed by his spiritual power, by his devotion to learning and wisdom, by his renunciation, the watchword of his life, nay, watered even by the flow of his own life-blood.... It is, therefore, that even his memory is sacred to us! ...

There are evils as well.... The priest naturally says to himself, "Why should I part with the power that has made the deities subservient to me, has given me mastery over physical and mental illness, and has gained for me the services of ghosts, demons and other unseen spirits? I have dearly bought this power by the price of extreme renunciation. Why should I give to others that, to get which I had to give up wealth, name, fame, in short, all my earthly comforts and happiness?" Again, that power is entirely mental. And how many opportunities are there for keeping it a perfect secret! Entangled in the wheel of circumstances, human nature becomes what it inevitably should be: being used to practise constant self-concealment, it becomes a victim of extreme selfishness and hypocrisy, and at last succumbs to the poisonous consequences which they bring in their train. In time, the reaction of this very desire to concealment redounds upon oneself. All knowledge, all wisdom is lost for want of proper exercise and diffusion; and what little remains is thought to have been obtained from some supernatural source; and, therefore, far from making fresh efforts to go in for originality and gain knowledge of new sciences, it is considered useless and futile to attempt to even improve the remnants of the old by cleansing them of their corruptions. Then lost to former wisdom, the former in domitable spirit of self-reliance, the priest, now glorifying himself merely in the name of his forefathers, mainly struggles to preserve untarnished for himself the same glory, the same privilege, the same veneration and the same supremacy as was enjoyed by his great forefathers. Consequently, his violent collision with the other castes. . . .

Having lost sight of the goal, drifting aimless, the priestly power is entangled, like the spider, in the web spun by itself. The chain that has been forged from generation to generation, with the greatest care, to be put on others' feet, is now tightened round its own in a thousand coils, and is thwarting its own movement in hundreds of ways. Caught in the endless thread of the net of infinite rites, ceremonies and customs, which it spread on all sides, as external means for purification of the body and the mind, with a view to keeping society in the iron grasp of these innumerable bonds—the priestly power, thus hopelessly entangled from head to foot, is now asleep in despair! There is no escaping out of it now. Tear the net and the priesthood of the priest is shaken to its foundation! There is implanted in every man, naturally, a strong desire for progress; and those, who, finding that the fulfilment of this desire is an impossibility so long as one is trammelled in the shackles of priesthood, rend this net and take to the profession of other castes in order to earn money thereby—them, the society immediately dispossesses of their priestly rights. Society has no faith in the Brahmananess of the so-called Brahmanas, who, instead of keeping the Shikhâ, part their hair, who, giving up their ancient habits and ancestral customs, clothe themselves in semi-European dress, and adopt the newly introduced usages, from the West, in a hybrid fashion. Again, in those parts of India, wherever this new-comer, the English Government, is introducing new modes of education and opening up new channels for the coming-in of wealth, there, hosts of Brahmana youths are giving up their hereditary priestly profession, and trying to earn their livelihood and become rich by adopting the callings of other castes, with the result, that the habits and customs of the priestly class, handed down from their distant forefathers, are scattered to the winds, and are fast disappearing from the land.... Even orthodox Pandits of the old school, undergoing pecuniary difficulties, are sending their sons to the colleges of the English Universities, or making them choose the callings of Vaidyas, Kâyasthas and other non-Brahmana castes. If the current of affairs goes on running in this course, then it is a question of most serious reflection, no doubt—how long more will the priestly class continue on India's soil. Those who lay the fault of attempting to bring down the supremacy of the priestly class at the door of any particular person, or body of persons other than themselves, ought to know that, in obedience to the inevitable Law of Nature, the Brahmana caste is erecting, with its own hands, its own sepulchre; and this is what ought to be. It is good and appropriate that every caste of high birth and privileged nobility should make it its principal duty to raise its own funeral pyre with its own hands.[5]

* * *

Priestcraft is the bane of India. Can man degrade his brother and himself escape degradation? . . . Can one injure anyone without injuring himself? The mass of Brahmana and Kshatriya tyranny has recoiled upon their own heads with compound interest; and a thousand years of slavery and degradation is what the inexorable law of Karma is visiting upon them.[6]

My brother, what experiences I have had in the South, of the upper classes torturing the lower.... Is it religion that fails to remove the misery of the poor and turn man into gods! Do you think our religion is worth the name? Ours is only 'Dont-touchism,' only "Touch me not," "Touch me not." Good heavens! A country, the big leaders of which have for the last two thousand years been only discussing whether to take food with the right hand or the left, whether to take water from the right hand side or the left,...if such a country does not go to ruin what other will?... A country where millions of people live on flowers of the *Mohua* plant, and a million or two of Sadhus and a hundred million or so of Brahmanas suck the blood of these poor people, without even the least effort for their amelioration—is that a country or hell? Is that a religion or the devil's dance? My brother, here is one thing for you to understand fully—I have travelled all over India, and seen this country too—can there be an effect without cause? Can there be punishment without sin?[7]

Sitting down these hundreds of years with an ever-increasing load of crystallised superstition on your heads, for hundreds of years spending all your energy upon discussing the touchableness or untouchableness of this food or that, with all humanity crushed out of you by the continuous social tyranny of ages—what are you? ... Come, be men! Kick out the priests who are always against progress, because they would never mend. Their hearts would never become big. They are the offspring of centuries of superstition and tyranny. Root out priestcraft first. Come, be men! Come out of your narrow holes and have a look abroad. See how nations are on the march! ... A race of dotards, you lose your caste if you come out![8]

We must travel, we must go to foreign parts. We must see how the engine of society works in other countries and keep free and open communications with what is going on in the minds of other nations, if we really want to be a nation again. And over and above all, we must cease to tyrannise.[9]

Ah tyrants! You do not know that the obverse is tyranny and the reverse, slavery. The slave and the tyrant are synonymous.[10]

The tyranny of the minority is the worst tyranny in the world.[11]

The masses who comprise the lowest caste, through ages of constant tyranny of the higher castes and by being treated by them with blows and kicks at every step they took, have totally lost their manliness and become like professional beggars.[12]

Who reduced the Bhângis and the Pariahs to their present degraded condition? Heartlessness in our behaviour and at the same time preaching wonderful Advaitism—is it not adding insult to injury?[13]

To what a ludicrous state we are brought! If a Bhângi comes to anybody as a Bhângi he would be shunned as the plague; but no sooner does he get a cupful of water poured upon his head with some mutterings of prayer by a Padri, and get a coat on his back, no matter how threadbare, and come into the room of the most orthodox Hindu—I don't see the man who then dare refuse him a chair and a hearty shake of the hands!! Irony can go no farther. And come and see what they, the Padris, are doing here in the South. They are converting the lower classes by lakhs; and in Travancore, the most priest-ridden country in India—where every bit of land is owned by the Brahmanas ...nearly one-fourth has become Christians! And I cannot blame them; what part have they in David and what in Jesse? When, when, O Lord, shall man be brother to man?[14]

* * *

Priestcraft is in its nature cruel and heartless. That is why religion goes down where priestcraft arises. Says Vedanta, we must give up the idea of privilege, then will religion come. Before that there is no religion at all.[15]

The Vedanta was (and is) the boldest system of religion. It stopped nowhere, and it had one advantage. There was no body of priests who sought to suppress every man who tried to tell the truth. There was always absolute religious freedom. In India, the bondage of superstition is a social one.[16]

The idea of privilege is the bane of human life. Two forces, as it were, are constantly at work, one making caste, and the other breaking down privilege. And whenever privilege is broken down, more and more light and progress come to a race. . . . None can be Vedantists, and at the same time admit of privilege to any one, either mental, physical or spiritual; absolutely no privilege for anyone. The same power is in every man, the one manifesting more, the other less; the same potentiality is in everyone. . . . The idea that one man is born superior to another has no meaning in the Vedanta.[17]

Caste is a natural order. I can perform one

duty in social life, and you another: you can govern a country, and I can mend a pair of old shoes; but that is no reason why you are greater than I, for can you mend my shoes? Can I govern the country? I am clever in mending shoes, you are clever in reading Vedas; but that is no reason why you should trample on my head; why if one commits murder should he be praised, and if another steals an apple why should he be hanged! This will have to go. Caste is good. That is the only natural way of solving life. Men must form themselves into groups, and you cannot get rid of that. Wherever you go, there will be caste. But that does not mean that there should be these privileges. They should be knocked on the head.... It is in the nature of society to form itself into groups; and what will go will be these privileges! ... If you teach Vedanta to the fisherman, he will say, "I am as good a man as you; I am a fisherman, you are a philosopher; but I have the same God in me, as you have in you." And that is what we want, no privilege for any one, equal chances for all; let everyone be taught that the Divine is within and every one will work out his salvation.[18]

Thus, trampling on every privilege and

everything in us that works for privilege, let us work for that knowledge which will bring the feeling of sameness towards all mankind.[19]

* * *

Two forces seem to be working throughout nature. One of these is constantly differentiating, and the other is as constantly unifying: the one making more and more for separate individuals, the other, as it were, bringing the individuals into a mass, bringing out sameness in the midst of all these differenciations.... It is urged that even in the physical body and social classification absolute sameness would produce natural death and social death.... Sameness, therefore, is to be avoided.... Practically, it is the same argument which is urged by the Brahmanas of India, when they want to uphold the divisions and castes, when they want to uphold the privileges of a certain portion of the community against everybody else. The destruction of caste, they declare, would lead to destruction of society, and boldly they produce the historical fact, that theirs has been the longest-lived society.

On the other hand, the idea of oneness has had its advocates throughout all times.... The Vedantist declares that unity is the only thing that exists, variety is but phenomenal, ephemeral and apparent. "Look not to variety," says the Vedantist, "go back to unity." . . . This is a fact that variation exists, and so it must if life is to be. This is also a fact that in and through these variations unity must be perceived. . . .

The whole universe is a play of unity in variety. . . . We cannot take one without granting the other. . . . That is the peculiar claim—not that this unity has to be made, but that it already exists, and that you could not perceive the variety at all without it. God is not to be made, but He already exists. . . . We cannot deny that this is the real idea; yet at the same time comes the difficulty that the sameness as regards external forms and position can never be attained. But what can be attained is elimination of privilege. That is really the work before the whole world. In all social lives, there has been that one fight in every race, and in every country. The difficulty is not that one body of men are naturally more intelligent than another, but whether this body of men, because they have the advantage of intelligence, should take away even physical enjoyment from those who do not possess that advantage. The fight is to destroy that privilege. . . . That some people through natural aptitude, should be able to accumulate more wealth than others, is natural; but that on account of this power to acquire wealth they should tyrannise, and ride roughshod over those who cannot acquire so much wealth, is not a part of the law; and the fight has been against that. The enjoyment of advantage over another is privilege; and throughout ages, the aim of morality has been its destruction. This is the work that tends towards sameness, towards unity, without destroying variety.[20]

Potentially each one of us has that infinite ocean of Existence, Knowledge and Bliss as our birthright, our real nature; and the difference between us is caused by the greater or lesser power to manifest that divine. Therefore the Vedanta lays down that each man should be treated not as what he manifests, but as what he stands for. Each human being stands for the divine, and therefore every teacher should be helpful, not by condemning man, but by helping him to call forth the divinity that is within him.[21]

And this has mostly to be done by the Brahmanas themselves, because it is the duty of every aristocracy to dig its own grave; and the sooner it does so, the better for all. No time should be lost.[22]

I regret that in modern times there should be so much discussion (dissension ?) between castes. This must stop. It is useless on both sides, especially on the side of the higher caste, the Brahmana, because the day for these privileges and exclusive claims is gone. The duty of every aristocracy is to dig its own grave, and the sooner it does so the better. The more it delays, the more it will fester and the worse death it will die. It is the duty of the Brahmana, therefore, to work for the salvation of the rest of mankind, in India. If he does that and so long as he does that, he is a Brahmana; but he is not a Brahmana when he goes about making money.[23]

IV

FALSE GODS

Here I shall say something about food regulations. All the old customs have faded away, and nothing but a vague notion of not eating with this man and not eating with that man has been left among our countrymen. Purity by touch is the only relic left of the good rules laid down hundreds of years ago. Three kinds of food are forbidden in the Shâstras. First, the food that is by its very nature defective, as garlic or onions.... Secondly, food contaminated by external impurities.... Thirdly, we should avoid food touched by a wicked man, because contact with such produces bad ideas in us.... But the spirit of these observances is gone. What is left is this, that we cannot eat from the hands of any man who is not of the highest caste, even though he be the most wise and holy person. The disregard of those old rules is ever to be found in the confectioner's shop. If you look there, you will find flies hovering all over the confectionery, and the dust from the road blowing upon the sweetmeats, and the confectioner himself in a dress that is not very clean and neat.... Now the real spirit of this observance of purity about food is lost and the letter only remains. Thieves, drunkards and criminals can be our caste-fellow; but if a good and noble man eats food with a person of a lower caste, who is quite as respectable as himself, he will be outcasted and lost for ever. This custom has been the bane of our country.[1]

There is a celebrated verse in the Shrutis, "When food (Ahâra) is pure, then the Sattva becomes pure; when the Sattva is pure, then the Smriti"—the memory of the Lord, or the memory of our own perfection...—"becomes truer, steadier and absolute." Ramanuja takes this word, Ahâra, to mean food; and he has made it one of the turning-points of his philosophy.... Shankaracharya...says, this word, Ahâra, means thought collected in the mind... Both are necessary.... But the defect is, that in modern India we have forgotten the advice of Shankaracharya and taken only the "pure food" meaning. That is why people get mad with me when I say, "Religion has got into the kitchen"; and if you had been in Madras with me, you would have agreed with me. The Bengalees are better than that. In Madras, they throw away food if anybody looks at it. And with all this I do not see that the people are any the better there. If only eating this or that sort of food, and saving it from the look of this person and that person would give them perfection, you would expect them all to be perfect men, which they are not.[2]

Shankaracharya has said that the word Ahâra ... means "objects of the senses," whereas Sri Ramanuja has taken the meaning of Ahâra to be "food." In my opinion we should take that meaning of the word which reconciles both these points of view. Are we to pass our lives discussing all the time about the purity and impurity of the food only, or are we to practise the restraining of our senses? Surely, the restraining of the senses is the main object; and the discrimination of good and bad, pure and impure foods, only helps one, to a certain extent, in gaining that end. There are, according to our Scriptures, three things which make food impure: (i) Jâti-dosha or natural defects of a certain class of food, like onions, garlic, etc.; (ii) Nimitta-dosha, or defects arising from the presence of external impurities in it, such as dead insects, dust, etc., that attach to sweetmeats bought in shops; (iii) Ashraya-dosha, or defects that arise by the food coming from evil sources, as when it has been touched and handled by wicked persons. Special care should be taken to avoid the first and second classes of defects. But, in this country, men pay no regard to these very two, and go on fighting for the third alone, the very one that none but a Yogi could really discriminate![3]

There is danger of our religion getting into the kitchen. We are neither Vedantists, most of us now, nor Pauranics, nor Tantrics. We are just "Don't-touchists." Our religion is in the kitchen. Our God is the cooking-pot, and our religion is—"Don't touch me, I am holy." If this goes on for another century, every one of us will be in a lunatic asylum.[4]

* * *

There is a cry nowadays about this and that food, and about Varnâshrama; and the Bengalees are the most vociferous in these cries. I would ask every one of you, what do you know about this Varnâshrama? Where are the four castes to-day in this country? Answer me! I do not see the four castes. Just as our Bengalee proverb has it, "A headache without a head," so you want to make this Varnâshrama here. There are not four castes here. I see only Brahmana and the Shudra. If there are the Kshatriyas and Vaishyas, where are they and why do not you Brahmanas order them to take the Yajnopavita and study the Vedas, as every Hindu ought to do?—and if the Vaishya and the Kshatriyas do not exist, but only the Brahmanas and the Shudras, the Shâstras say, that the Brahmana must not live in a country where there are only Shudras; so depart bag and baggage! Do you know what the Shâstras say about people who have been eating Mlechchha food, and living under a Government of the Mlechchhas, as you have for the last thousand years? Do you know the penance for that? The penance would be burning oneself with one's own hands. Do you want to pass as teachers, and walk like hypocrites? ... You do not believe in your own Shastras and yet want to make others believe in them. If you think you are not able to do that in this age, admit your weakness and excuse the weakness of others, take the other castes up, give them a helping hand, let them study the Vedas and become just as good Aryans as any other Aryans in the world; and be you likewise Aryans, you Brahmanas of Bengal![5]

The caste we have now is not that of seven hundred years ago. Every blow has riveted it.[6]

Do you not see that nowhere in India now are the original four castes of Brahmanas, Kshatriyas, Vaishyas and Shudras as of old. The numberless modern subdivisions of the Brahmanas that split them up into so many castes, as it were, have to be abolished and a single Brahmana caste to be made by uniting them all. Each of the three remaining castes also will have to be brought similarly into single groups, as was the case in the Vedic times. Without this, will the Motherland be really benefited by your simply crying, as you do nowadays, "We won't touch you!" "We won't take him back into our caste!" Never my boy![7]

No man, no nation, my son, can hate others and live. India's doom was sealed the very day they invented the word Mlechchha and stopped from communion with others. Take care how you foster that idea. It is good to talk glibly about Vedanta, but how hard to carry out even its least precepts![8]

In our country we hear much about some people belonging to the gentry and some to the lower classes. But in the eyes of the Government all are *natives* without exception. Maharajas, Rajas, Brahmanas, Kshatriyas, Vaishyas, Shudras—all belong to the same class—that of natives. The law, and the test which applies to coolies, is applicable to all natives without distinction. Thanks to you, O English Government! Through your grace, for a moment at least, I feel myself one with the whole body of natives.... Nowadays we hear it from the lips of people of all castes in India that they are all full-blooded Aryans—only there is difference of opinion amongst them about the exact percentage of Aryan blood in their veins, some claiming to have the full measure of it, while others may have an ounce more or less than another—that is all.... And they have come to this country out of humanitarian principles, like the English.... Their religion also is of the same pattern as that of the English! And their forefathers looked just like the English; only living under the tropical sun of India has turned them black! Now, come forward with your pretensions, if you dare! "You are all natives," the Government says. Among that mass of black, a shade deeper or lighter cannot be distinguished. The Government says, "They are all natives."...

Out with these differences of white and black, and this nicety about the proportion of Aryan blood among the natives! How awkward it looks for slaves to be over-fastidious about pedigrees! There was a Dom (Pariah) who used to say, "You won't find anywhere on earth a caste superior to ours. You must know we are Dom-m-m-s!" But do you see the fun of it? The excesses about caste distinctions obtain most among people who are least honoured among mankind.[9]

What shall I say of India? Let alone her Shudra class—her Brahmanas, to whom belonged the acquisition of scriptural knowledge, are now the foreign professors; her Kshatriyas the ruling Englishmen; and Vaishyas too, the English, in whose bone and marrow is the instinct of trade ; so that, only the Shudraness—the beast-of-burdenness—is now left with the Indians themselves. A cloud of impenetrable darkness has at present equally enveloped us all.... What to speak separately of the distinct Shudra class of such a land, where the whole population has virtually come down to the level of the Shudra?[10]

I do not advise our inter-marriage with nations professing an alien religion. At least for the present, that will, of a certainty, slacken the ties of society, and be a cause of manifold mischief. It is the inter-marriage between people of the same religion that I advocate.

The time is yet (24th January, 1898) very long in coming when marriages of that kind will be widely possible. Besides, it is not judicious now to go in for that, all of a sudden. One of the secrets of work is to go by the way of the least possible resistance. So, first of all, let there be marriages within the sphere of one's caste-people. Take for instance, the Kâyasthas of Bengal. They have several subdivisions among them, such as, the *Uttara-rârhi*, *Dakshina-rârhi*, *Bangaja*, etc., and they do not inter-marry with each other. Now, let there be inter-marriages between the *Uttara-rârhis* and the *Dakshina-rârhis*, and if that is not possible at present, let it be between the *Bangajas* and the *Dakshina-rârhis*. Thus we are to build up that which is already existing, and which is in our hands to reduce into practice—reform does not mean wholesale breaking down....

Don't you see how in our society, marriage being restricted for several hundreds of years within the same subdivisions of each caste, has come to such a pass nowadays as virtually to mean marital alliance between cousins and near relations; and how for this very reason the race is getting deteriorated physically; and consequently all sorts of disease and other evils are finding a ready entrance into it? The blood, having had to circulate within the narrow circle of a limited number of individuals, has become vitiated; so the new-born children inherit from their very birth the constitutional diseases of their fathers. Thus, born with poor blood, their bodies have very little power to resist the microbes of any disease, which are ever ready to prey upon them. It is only by widening the circle of marriage that we can infuse a new and a different kind of blood into our progeny, so that they may be saved from the clutches of many of our present-day diseases and other consequent evils.[11]

* * *

Here naturally comes the difficult and the vexed question of caste and social reformation, which has been uppermost for centuries in the minds of our people. I must frankly tell you that I am neither a caste-breaker nor a mere social reformer. I have nothing to do directly with your castes or with your social reformation. Live in any caste you like; but that is no reason why you should hate another man or another caste. It is love and love alone that I preach, and I base my teaching on the great Vedantic truth of the sameness and omnipresence of the Soul of the Universe.[12]

We are orthodox Hindus; but we refuse to identify ourselves with "Don't-touchism." That is not Hinduism: it is in none of our books; it is an unorthodox superstition which has interfered with national efficiency all along the line.[13]

B— has sent me a book written by S—. From a perusal of that work B— has come to know that all the people of this world are impure, and that they are by their very nature debarred from having a jot of religion; that only the handful of Brahmanas that are in India have the sole right to it, and among these again, S— and B— are the sun and moon, so to speak. Bravo! What a powerful religion indeed! In Bengal specially, that sort of religion is very easy to practise. There is no easier way than that. The whole truth about austerities and spiritual exercises is, in a nutshell, that I am pure and all the rest are impure! A beastly, demoniac, hellish religion this![14]

We have brains, but no hands. We have the doctrine of Vedanta, but we have not the power to reduce it into practice. In our books there is the doctrine of universal equality; but in work we make great distinctions. It was in India that unselfish and disinterested work of the most exalted type was preached; but in practice we are awfully cruel, awfully heartless —unable to think of anything besides our own mass-of-flesh bodies.[15]

Death lies in the senses. Life on the plane of the spirit is the only life, life on the other plane is mere death. The whole of this life can be only described as a gymnasium. We must go beyond it to enjoy real life. As long as "Touch-me-not-ism" is your creed and the kitchen-pot your deity, you cannot rise spirit-country. They are the backbone of the coun-ually.[16]

Alas! nobody thinks of the poor of the try, who by their labour are producing food—these people, the sweepers and labourers, who, if they stop work for one day, will create a panic in the town. But there is none to sympathise with them, none to console them in their misery. Just see, for want of sympathy from the Hindus, thousands of Pariahs in Madras are turning Christians. Don't think this is simply due to the pinch of hunger; it is because they do not get any sympathy from us. We are day and night calling out to them, "Don't touch us! Don't touch us!" Is there any compassion or kindliness of heart in the country? Only a class of "Don't-touchists"; kick such customs out! I sometimes feel the urge to break the barriers of "Don't-touchism," go at once and call out, "Come all who are poor, miserable, wretched and downtrodden," and to bring them all together in the name of Sri Ramakrishna. Unless they rise, the Mother won't awaken.... Let us open their eyes—I see clear as daylight that there is the one Brahman in all, in them and me—one Shakti dwells in all. The only difference is of manifestation. Unless the blood circulates over the whole body, has any country risen at any time? If one limb is paralysed, then even with the other limbs whole, not much can be done with that body—know this for certain....

After so much austerity I have understood this as the real truth—God is present in every Jiva; there is no other God besides that. "Who serves Jiva, serves God indeed."[17]

* * *

Aye, in this country of ours, the very birthplace of the Vedanta, our masses have been hypnotised for ages into that state. To touch them is pollution, to sit with them is pollution! Hopeless they are born, hopeless they must remain! And the result is that they have been sinking, sinking, sinking, and have come to the last stage to which a human being can come. For what country is there in the world where man has to sleep with the cattle; and for this, blame nobody else; do not commit the mistake of the ignorant. The effect is here, and the cause is here too. We are to blame. Stand up, be bold, and take the blame on your own shoulders. Do not go about throwing mud at others; for all the faults you suffer from, you are the sole and only cause.[18]

The country from end to end is being bored to extinction by the cries, "Don't touch," "Don't touch," of the non-touchism party. In that exclusive circle of theirs, too, there is no discrimination of good and bad man, for there food may be taken from the hands of anyone who wears a thread round his neck and calls himself a Brahmana! ... Your religion seems nowadays to be confined to the cooking-pot alone. You put on one side the sublime truths of religion and fight, as they say, for the skin of the fruit and not for the fruit itself! .... Now, look here! You being a Brahmana of a certain class, say of the Bhattacharya class, why should you not eat rice cooked by Brahmanas of all classes? Why should you, who belong to the Râhri section, object to take rice cooked by a Brahmana of the Vârendra section, or why should a Vârendra object to taking your rice? Again, why should not the other sub-castes in the West and the South of India, e.g., the Mahratta, Telinga, Kanouji, do the same? Do you not see that hundreds of Brahmanas and Kâyasthas in Bengal now go secretly to eat dainties in public restaurants, and when they come out of these places pose as leaders of society and frame rules to support "dont-touchism!" Must our society really be guided by laws dictated by such hypocrites? No, I say. On the contrary, we must turn them out. The laws laid down by the great Rishis of old must be brought back and be made to rule supreme once more. Then alone can national well-being be ours.[19]

Well, do you think there is any religion left in India! The paths of knowledge, devotion and Yoga—all have gone, and now there remains only that of "Don't-touchism"—"Don't touch me," "Don't touch me!" The whole world is impure, and I am pure! Lucid Brahma-jnâna! Bravo! Great God! Nowadays Brahman is neither in the recesses of the heart, nor in the highest heaven, nor in all beings—now He is in the cooking-pot. Formerly the characteristic of a noble-minded man was "त्रिभुवनमुपकारश्रेणिभिः प्रीयमाणः—to please the whole universe by one's numerous acts of service;"

but now it is—I am pure and the whole world is impure—go and get money, and set it at my feet.[20]

If anybody is born of a low caste in our country he is gone for ever, there is no hope for him. Why, what a tyranny it is! There are possibilities, opportunities and hope for every individual in this country (U.S.A.). To-day he is poor, to-morrow he may become rich and learned and respected. Here (in U.S.A.) every one is anxious to help the poor. In India there is a howling cry that we are very poor, but how many charitable associations are there for the well-being of the poor! How many people really weep for the sorrows and sufferings of the millions of poor in India? Are we men? What are we doing for their livelihood, for their improvement? We do not touch them, we avoid their company! Are we men? Those thousands of Brahmanas—what are they doing for the low, downtrodden masses of India? "Don't touch," "Don't touch," is the only phrase that plays upon their lips! How mean and degraded has our eternal religion become at their hands! Wherein does our religion lie now? In "Don't-touchism" alone, and nowhere else![21]

A dreadful slough is in front of you—take

care; many fall into it and die. The slough is this, that the present religion of the Hindus is not in the Vedas, nor in the Puranas, nor in Bhakti, nor in Mukti—religion has entered into the cooking-pot. The present religion of the Hindus is neither the path of Knowledge, nor that of Reason—it is "Don't-touchism."—"Don't touch me!" "Don't touch me!"—that exhausts its description. See that you do not lose your lives in this dire irreligion of "Don't-touchism." Must the teaching "आत्मवत् सर्वभूतेषु"—Looking upon all beings as your own self"—be confined to books alone? How will they grant salvation who cannot feed a hungry mouth with a crumb of bread? How will those who become impure at the mere breath of others, purify others? "Don't-touchism" is a form of mental disease. Beware! All expansion is life, all contraction is death. All love is expansion, all selfishness is contraction. Love is, therefore, the only law of life.[22]

V

AVOID STRIFE

Modern caste distinction is a barrier to India's progress. It narrows, restricts, separates. It will crumble before the advance of ideas.[1]

I fully agree with the educated classes in India, that a thorough overhauling of society is necessary; but how to do it? The destructive plans of reformers have failed. My plan is this. We have not done badly in the past, certainly not. Our society is not bad but good, only I want it to be better still.... Take the case of caste, in Sanskrit, Jâti, i.e., species. Now, this is the idea of creation.... So long as any species is vigorous and active it must throw out varieties. When it ceases or is stopped from breeding varieties, it dies. Now, the original idea of Jâti was this freedom of the individual to express his nature, his Prakriti, his Jâti, his caste; and so it remained for thousands of years. Not even in the latest books is inter-dining prohibited; nor in any of the older books is inter-marriage forbidden. Then what was the cause of India's downfall?—the giving up of this idea of caste. As the Gita says, with the extinction of caste the world will be destroyed. . . . The present caste is not the real Jâti, but a hindrance to its progress. It really has prevented the free action of Jâti, i.e., caste variation. Any crystallised custom or privilege or hereditary class in any shape really prevents caste (Jâti) from having its full sway; and whenever any nation ceases to produce this immense variety, it must die.... Every frozen aristocracy or privileged class is a blow to caste and is not caste. Let Jâti have its sway; break down every barrier in the way of caste and we shall rise.... Every Hindu knows that Astrologers try to fix the caste of every boy or girl as soon as he or she is born. That is the real caste—the individuality ; and Jyotish (Astrology) recognises that. And we can only rise by giving it full sway again. This variety does not mean inequality, nor any special privilege.[2]

The Brahmanahood is the ideal of humanity in India, as wonderfully put forward by Shankaracharya at the beginning of his commentary on the Gita, where he speaks about the reason for Krishna's coming as a preacher for the preservation of Brahmanahood, or

Brahmananess. That was the great end. This Brahmana, the man of God, he who has known Brahman, the ideal man, the perfect man, must remain; he must not go. And with all the defects of the caste now, we know that we must all be ready to give to the Brahmana his credit, that from them have come more men with real Brahmananess in them than from all the other castes. We must be bold enough, must be brave enough to speak of their defects; but at the same time we must give the credit that is due to them.... Therefore, my friends, it is no use fighting among castes. What good will it do? It will divide us all the more, degrade us all the more.[3]

To the non-Brahmana castes I say, be not in a hurry, do not seize every opportunity of fighting the Brahmana, because, as I have shown, you are suffering from your own fault. Who told you to neglect spirituality and Sanskrit learning? What have you been doing all this time? Why have you been indifferent? Why do you now fret and fume because somebody else had more brains, more energy, more pluck and go, than you! Instead of wasting your energies in vain discussions and quarrels in the newspapers, instead of fighting and quarrelling in your own homes—which is sinful—use all your energies in acquiring the culture which the Brahmana has, and the thing is done. Why do you not become Sanskrit scholars? Why do you not spend millions to bring Sanskrit education to all the castes in India? That is the question. The moment you do these things, you are equal to the Brahmana. That is the secret of power in India. Sanskrit and prestige go together in India.[4]

The only safety, I tell you men who belong to the lower castes, the only way to raise your condition, is to study Sanskrit, and this fighting and writing and frothing against the higher castes is in vain; it does no good, and it creates fight and quarrel; and this race, unfortunately already divided, is going to be divided more and more. The only way to bring about the levelling of caste is to appropriate the culture, the education, which is the strength of the higher castes. That done, you have what you want.[5]

It is culture that withstands shocks, not a simple mass of knowledge.... We all know, in modern times, of nations which have masses of knowledge; but what of them? They are like tigers, they are like savages, because culture is not there. Knowledge is only skin-deep, as civilisation is; and a little scratch brings out the old savage; such things happen; this is the danger. Teach the masses in the vernaculars, give them ideas, they will get information; but something more is necessary, give them culture. Until you give them that there can be no permanence in the raised condition of the masses.[6]

* * *

To the Brahmanas I appeal, that they must work hard to raise the Indian people by teaching them what they know, by giving out the culture that they have accumulated for centuries. It is clearly the duty of the Brahmanas of India to remember what real Brahmanahood is. As Manu says, all these privileges and honours are given to the Brahmana because, "with him is the treasury of virtue." He must open that treasury and distribute its valuables to the world. It is true that he was the earliest preacher to the Indian races, he was the first to renounce everything in order to attain to the higher realisation of life, before others could reach to the idea. It was not his fault that he reached ahead of the other castes.... But it is one thing to gain advantage, and another thing to preserve it for evil use. Whenever power is used for evil it becomes diabolical; it must be used for good only. So this accumulated culture of ages of which the Brahmana has been the trustee he must now give to the people at large; and it was because he did not give it to the people, that the Mohammedan invasion was possible. It was because he did not open this Treasury to the people from the beginning, that for a thousand years we have been trodden under the heels of every one who chose to come to India; it was through that we have become degraded, and the first task must be to break open the cells that hide the wonderful treasures which our common ancestors accumulated; bring them out, and give them to everybody; and the Brahmana must be the first to do it. There is an old superstition in Bengal that if the cobra that bites, sucks out his own poison from the patient, the man must survive. Well then, the Brahmana must suck out his own poison.[7]

The super-arrogated excellence of birth of any caste in India is only pure myth, and in no part of India has it, we are sorry to say, found such congenial soil owing to linguistic differences as in the South.... We believe in Indian caste as one of the greatest social institutions that the Lord gave to man. We also believe that though the unavoidable defects, foreign persecutions and, above all, the monumental ignorance and pride of many Brahmanas who do not deserve the name, have thwarted, in many ways, the legitimate fructification of this most glorious Indian Institution, it has already worked wonders for the land of Bharata and is destined to lead Indian humanity to its goal....

Any one who claims to be a Brahmana, then, should prove his pretensions first by manifesting that spirituality and next by raising others to the same status. On the face of this it seems that most of them are only nursing a false pride of birth, and any schemer, native or foreign, who can pander to this vanity and inherent laziness, by fulsome sophistry, appears to satisfy most. Beware Brahmanas, this is the sign of death! Arise and show your manhood, your Brahmanahood, by raising the non-Brahmanas around you—not in the spirit of a master, not with the rotten canker of egotism crawling with superstitions and the charlatanry of East and West—but in the spirit of a servant. For verily he who knows how to serve knows how to rule. The non-Brahmanas also have been spending their energy in kindling the fire of caste hatred —vain and useless to solve the problem—to which every non-Hindu is only too glad to throw on a load of fuel. Not a step forward can be made by these inter-caste quarrels, not one difficulty removed; only the beneficent onward march of events would be thrown back, possibly for centuries, if the fire bursts out into flame.[8]

* * *

It is true that the caste-system becomes essential in the ordinary course of nature. Those that have aptitudes for a particular work form a class. But who is to settle the class of a particular individual? If a Brahmana thinks that he has a special aptitude for spiritual culture, why should he be afraid to meet a Shudra in an open field? Will a horse be afraid of running a race with a jade?[9]

Every action that helps a being manifest its divine nature more and more is good, every action that retards it is evil. The only way of getting our divine nature manifested is by helping others to do the same. If there is inequality in nature, still there must be equal chance for all—or if greater for some and for some less—the weaker should be given more chance than the strong. In other words, a Brahmana is not so much in need of education as a Chandala. If the son of a Brahmana needs one teacher, that of a Chandala needs ten. For greater help must be given to him whom nature has not endowed with an acute intellect from birth. It is a mad man who carries coal to Newcastle. The poor, the downtrodden, the ignorant, let these be your God.[10]

Our aristocratic ancestors went on treading the common masses of our country under foot, till they became helpless, till under this torment the poor, poor people nearly forgot that they were human beings.... With all our boasted education of modern times, if anybody says a kind word for them, I often find our men shrinking at once from the duty of lifting them up, these poor downtrodden people. Not only so, but I also find that all sorts of most demoniacal and brutal arguments, culled from the crude ideas of hereditary transmission and other such gibberish from the Western world, are brought forward in order to brutalise and tyrannise over the poor, all the more.... Aye, Brahmanas, if the Brahmana has more aptitude for learning on the ground of heredity than the Pariah, spend no more money on the Brahmana's education, but spend all on the Pariah. Give to the weak, for there all the gift is needed. If the Brahmana is born clever, he can educate himself without help. If the others are not born clever, let them have all the teaching and the teachers they want. This is justice and reason as I understand it. Our poor people, these downtrodden masses of India, therefore, require to hear and to know what they really are. Aye, let every man and woman and child, without respect of caste or birth, weakness or strength, hear and learn that behind the strong and the weak, behind the high and the low, behind every one, there is that Infinite Soul, assuring the infinite possibility and the infinite capacity of all to become great and good. Let us proclaim to every soul—"Arise, awake, and stop not till the goal is reached." Arise, awake! Awake from this hypnotism of weakness! None is really weak; the soul is infinite, omnipotent and omniscient. Stand up, assert yourself, proclaim the God within you; do not deny Him![11]

Our mission is for the destitute, the poor, and the illiterate peasantry and labouring classes; and if after everything has been done for them first, there is spare time, then only for the gentry. Those peasants and labouring people will be won over by love.... "One must raise oneself by one's own exertions"—this holds good in all spheres. We help them to help themselves.... The moment they will come to understand their own condition and feel the necessity of help and improvement, know that your work is taking effect and is in the right direction. While the little good that the moneyed classes, out of pity, do to the poor, does not last; and ultimately it does nothing but harm to both parties. The peasants and labouring classes are in a moribund condition; so what is needed is that the moneyed people will only help them to regain their vitality, and nothing more. Then leave the peasants and labourers to look to their own problems, to grapple with and solve it. But then you must take care not to set up class-strife between the poor peasants, the labouring people and the wealthy classes.[12]

VI

I AM A SOCIALIST

The four castes, Brahmana, Kshatriya, Vaishya and Shudra, . . . in succession, rule the world. During the period of supreme authority exercised by each of these castes, some acts are accomplished, which conduce to the welfare of the people, while others are injurious to them.[1]

As the priest is busy about centralising all knowledge and learning at a common centre, to wit, himself, so the king is ever up and doing in collecting all the earthly powers and focussing them in a central point. i.e., his own self. Of course, both are beneficial to society. At one time they are both needed for the common good of society but that is only at its infant stage.[2]

The king, the centre of the forces of the aggregate of his subjects, soon forgets that those forces are only stored with him so that he may increase and give them back a thousandfold in their potency, with the result that they may spread over the whole community for its good. Attributing all godship to himself, in his pride, like the king Vena, he looks upon other people as wretched specimens of humanity who should grovel before him; any opposition to his will, whether good or bad, is a great sin on the part of his subjects. Hence oppression steps into the place of protection—sucking their blood in place of preservation. . . . Where the society is healthy and strong there soon follows a fierce contest between the king and his subjects; and, by its reaction and convulsion, are flung away the sceptre and the crown, and the throne and the royal paraphernalia become like past curiosities preserved in the museum galleries.

As the result of this contest—as its reaction—is the appearance of the mighty power of the Vaishya, before whose angry glance the crowned heads, the lords of heroes, tremble like an aspen leaf on their thrones—whom the poor as well as the prince humbly follow in vain expectation of the golden jar in his hands, that like Tantalus' fruit always recedes from the grasp. . . . The power of the Vaishya lies in the possession of that coin, the charm of whose clinking sound works with an irresistible fascination on the minds of the four castes. The Vaishya is always in fear lest the Brahmana swindles him out of this, his only possession, and lest the Kshatriya usurps it by virtue of his superior strength of arms. For self-preservation the Vaishyas, as a body, are, therefore, of one mind. ... That the royal power may not anyhow stand in the way of the inflow of his riches, the merchant is ever watchful. But, for all that, he has never the least wish that the power should pass on from the kingly to the Shudra class. To what country does not the merchant go? Though himself ignorant, he, in carrying on his trade, transplants the learning, wisdom, art and science of one country to another. ...

And where are they, through whose physical labour only are possible, the influence of the Brahmana, the prowess of the Kshatriya, and the fortune of the Vaishya? What is their history, who, being the real body of society, are designated, at all times, in all countries, as "they—the base-born?" ... The Shudras of countries other than India have become, it seems a little awake; but they are wanting in proper education and have only the mutual hatred of men of their own class—a trait common to Shudras. What avails it if they greatly outnumber the other classes? That unity, by which ten men collect the strength of a million, is yet far away from the Shudra;

hence, according to the law of nature, the Shudras invariably form the subject race. . . .

Yet, a time will come, when there will be the rising of the Shudra class, *with their Shudra-hood:* that is to say, not like that as at present, when the Shudras are becoming great by acquiring the characteristic qualities of the Vaishya or the Kshatriya, but a time will come, when the Shudras of every country, with their inborn Shudra nature and habits—not becoming in essence Vaishya or Kshatriya, but remaining as Shudras—will gain absolute supremacy in every society. The first glow of the dawn of this new power has already begun to slowly break upon the Western world; and the thoughtful are at their wits' end to reflect upon the final issue of this fresh phenomenon. Socialism, Anarchism, Nihilism and like other sects, are the vanguard of the social revolution that is to follow. As the result of grinding pressure and tyranny, from time out of mind, the Shudras, as a rule, are either meanly servile, licking dog-like the feet of the higher class, or otherwise are as inhuman as brute beasts.

In spite of the spread of education in the West, there is a great hindrance in the way of the rising of the Shudra class; and that is the recognition of caste as determined by the inherence of more or less good or bad qualities. By this very qualitative caste-system which obtained in India in ancient days, the Shudra class was kept down, bound hand and foot. In the first place, scarcely any opportunity was given to the Shudra for the accumulation of wealth, or the earning of proper knowledge and education; to add to this disadvantage, if ever a man of extraordinary parts and genius were born of the Shudra class, the influential higher sections of the society forthwith showered titular honours on him and lifted him up to their own circle. His wealth and the power of his wisdom were employed for the benefit of an alien caste—and his own caste-people reaped no benefit of his attainments; and not only so, the good-for-nothing people, the scum and refuse of the higher castes, were cast off and thrown into the Shudra class to swell their number.

Vasishtha, Narada, Satyakama Jabala, Vyasa, Kripa, Drona, Karna and others of questionable parentage were raised to the position of a Brahmana or a Kshatriya, in virtue of their superior learning or valour; but it remains to be seen how, by these upliftings, the prostitute, maidservant, fisherman or the charioteer class was benefited. Again, on the other hand, the fallen from the Brahmana, the Kshatriya or the

Vaishya class were always brought down to fill the ranks of the Shudras.

In modern India, no one born of Shudra parents, be he a millionaire or a great Pandit, has ever the right to leave his own society, with the result that the power of his wealth, intellect or wisdom, remaining confined within his own caste limits, is being employed for the betterment of his own community. This hereditary caste-system of India, being thus unable to overstep its own bounds, is slowly but surely conducing to the advancement of the people moving within the same circle. The improvement of the lower classes of India will go on, in this way, so long as she will be under a Government dealing with its subjects irrespective of their caste and position.[3]

* * *

Human society is in turn governed by the four castes—the priests, the soldiers, the traders and the labourers.... Last will come the labourer (Shudra) rule. Its advantages will be the distribution of physical comforts—its disadvantages, (perhaps) the lowering of culture. There will be a great distribution of ordinary culture, but extraordinary geniuses will be less and less.

If it is possible to form a State in which the knowledge of the priest, the culture of the military, the distributive spirit of the commercial and the ideal of equality of the last can all be kept intact, minus their evils, it will be an ideal State. But is it possible?

Yet the first three have had their day. Now is the time for the last—they must have it—none can resist it. I do not know all the difficulties about the gold or silver standards (nobody seems to know much as to that); but this much I see that the gold standard has been making the poor poorer, and the rich richer. Bryan was right when he said, "We refuse to be crucified on a cross of gold." The silver standard will give the poor a better chance in this unequal fight. I am a socialist not because I think it is a perfect system, but half a loaf is better than no bread.

The other systems have been tried and found wanting. Let this one be tried—if nothing else, for the novelty of the thing. A redistribution of pain and pleasure is better than always the same persons having pains and pleasures. . . . Let every dog have his day in this miserable world.[4]

All the members of a society ought to have the same opportunity for obtaining wealth, education or knowledge.... Freedom in all matters, i e., advance towards Mukti, is the worthiest gain of man.... Those social rules which stand in the way of the unfoldment of this freedom are injurious; and steps should be taken to destroy them speedily. Those institutions should be encouraged by which men advance in the path of freedom.[5]

Remember that the nation lives in the cottage.[6]

The peasant, the shoemaker, the sweeper, and such other lower classes of India have much greater capacity for work and self-reliance than you. They have been silently working through long ages, and producing the entire wealth of the land, without a word of complaint. Very soon they will get above you in position. Gradually capital is drifting into their hands and they are not so much troubled with wants as you are. Modern education has changed your fashion, but new avenues of wealth lie yet undiscovered for want of the inventive genius. You have so long oppressed these forbearing masses; now is the time for their retribution. And you will become extinct in your vain search for employment, making it the be-all and end-all of your life!

If the labourers stop work, your supply of

food and clothes also stop. And you regard them as low-class people and vaunt about your own culture! Engrossed in the struggle for existence they had not the opportunity for the awakening of knowledge. They have worked so long uniformly like machines guided by human intelligence, and the clever educated section have taken the substantial part of the fruit of their labour. In every country this has been the case. But times have changed. The lower classes are generally awakening to this fact and making a united front against this, determined to exact their legitimate dues. . . . The upper classes will no longer be able to repress the lower, try they ever so much. The well-being of the higher classes now lies in helping the lower to get their legitimate rights.[7]

When the masses will wake up, they will come to understand your oppression on them and by a puff of their mouth you will be entirely blown off! It is they who have introduced civilisation amongst you; and it is they who will then pull it down. Think how at the hands of the Gauls the mighty ancient Roman civilisation crumbled into dust! Therefore I say, try to rouse these lower classes from slumber by imparting learning and culture to them. When they will awaken—and awaken one day they must—they also will not forget your good services to them and will remain grateful to you.[8]

How my heart ached to think of what we think of the poor, the low, in India. They have no chance, no escape, no way to climb up. . . They sink lower and lower every day, they feel the blows showered upon them by a cruel society, and they do not know whence the blow comes. They have forgotten that they too are men. And the result is slavery. Thoughtful people within the last few years have seen it, but unfortunately laid it at the door of the Hindu religion; and to them the only way of bettering is by crushing this grandest religion of the world. Hear me, my friend, I have discovered the secret through the grace of the Lord. Religion is not at fault. On the other hand, your religion teaches you that every being is only your own self multiplied. But it was the want of practical application, the want of sympathy—the want of heart. This state of things must be removed, not by destroying religion but by following the great teachings of the Hindu faith, and joining with it the wonderful sympathy of that logical development of Hinduism—Buddhism. . . . A hundred thousand men and women, fired with the zeal of holiness, fortified with eternal faith in the Lord, and nerved to Lion's courage by their sympathy for the poor and the fallen and the down-trodden, will go over the length and breadth of the land, preaching the gospel of salvation, the gospel of help, the gospel of social raising up—the gospel of equality.[9]

Your duty at present is to go from village to village, and make the people understand that mere sitting about idly won't do any more. Make them understand their real condition and say, "O ye brothers, all arise! Awake! How much longer would you remain asleep!" . . . So long the Brahmanas have monopolised religion; but since they cannot hold their ground against the strong tide of time, go and take steps so that one and all in the land may get that religion. Impress upon their minds that they have the same right to religion as the Brahmanas. Initiate all, even down to the Chandalas, in these fiery Mantras. Also instruct them, in simple words, about the necessities of life, and in trade, commerce, agriculture, etc. If you cannot do this, then fie upon your education and culture, and fie upon your studying the Vedas and Vedanta![10]

* * *

However much you may parade your descent

from Aryan ancestors and sing the glories of ancient India day and night, and however much you may be strutting in the pride of your birth, you, the upper classes of India—do you think you are alive? You are but mummies ten thousand years old! It is among those whom your ancestors despised as "walking carrions," that the little of vitality, there is still in India, is to be found; and it is you who are the real 'walking corpses'. Your houses, your furniture look like museum specimens, so lifeless and antiquated they are; and even an eye-witness of your manners and customs, your movements and modes of life, is inclined to think he is listening to a grandmother's tale!! When, even after making a personal acquaintance with you, one returns home, one seems to think one had been to visit the paintings in an Art Gallery! In this world of Maya, you are the real illusions, the mystery, the real mirage in the desert, you, the upper classes of India!! You represent the past tense, with all its varieties of form jumbled into one. That one still seems to see you at the present time, is nothing but a nightmare brought on by indigestion. You are the void, the unsubstantial nonentities of the future. Denizens of the Dreamland, why are you loitering any longer? Fleshless and bloodless skeletons of the deadbody of past India that you are—why do you not quickly reduce yourselves into dust and disappear in the air? Aye, in your bony fingers are some priceless rings of jewel treasured up by your ancestors and within the embrace of your stinking corpse are preserved a good many ancient treasure-chests. So long you have not had the opportunity to hand them over. Now under the British rule, in these days of free education and enlightenment, pass them on to your heirs, aye, do it as quickly as you can. You merge yourselves in the void and disappear, and let New India arise in your place. Let her arise—out of the peasant's cottage, grasping the plough, out of the huts of the fishermen, the cobbler and the sweeper. Let her spring from the grocer's shop, from beside the oven of the fritter-seller. Let her emerge from the factory, from marts and from markets. Let her emerge from the groves and forests, from hills and mountains. These common people have suffered oppression for thousands of years—suffered it without murmer, and as a result have got wonderful fortitude. They have suffered eternal misery, which has given them unflinching vitality. Living on a handful of oatmeal they can convulse the world; give them only half a piece of bread, and the whole world will not be big enough to contain their energy; they are endowed with the inexhaustible vitality of a Raktavija. And, besides, they have got the wonderful strength that comes of a pure and moral life, which is not to be found anywhere else in the world. Such peacefulness, such contentment, such love, such power of silent and incessant work, and such manifestation of lion's strength in times of action—where else will you find these? Skeletons of the past, there, before you, are your successors, the India that is to be. Throw those treasure-chests of yours and those jewelled rings among them—as soon as you can; and you—vanish into air, and be seen no more—only keep your ears open. No sooner will you disappear, than you will hear the inaugural shout of Renaissant India—ringing with the voice of a million thunders and reverberating throughout the universe—"Wah Guru Ki Fateh—victory to the Guru!"[11]

REFERENCES

The references are mostly to *The Complete Works* of Swami Vivekananda, published by the Advaita Ashrama, Mayavati. The fifth edition of the first two volumes, the fourth edition of the next three volumes, the third edition of the sixth volume, and the second edition of the seventh volume have been used. The Roman numbers refer to volumes of *The Complete Works*. The figures before the Roman numbers indicate the numbers of the quotations and those behind give the pages of the volumes.

CHAPTER 1

1. IV. 340; 2. IV. 242; 3. V. 426-27; 4. V. 427; 5. V. 427-28; 6. V. 435; 7. V. 438; 8. V. 438-39; 9. IV. 244; 10. IV. 242-44; 11. *Women of India*, 15-16; 12. III. 132-33; 13. V. 231; 14. III. 295-96; 15. V. 143-44; 16. V. 196; 17. V. 293; 18. V. 354-56; 19. V. 293; 20. V. 293; 21. V. 293; 22. VI. 177; 23. V. 352; 24. V. 353; 25. V. 357-59.

CHAPTER II

1. IV. 335-37; 2. V. 330; 3. III. 227; 4. V. 132; 5. III. 196-97; 6. VI. 302-3; 7. V. 27; 8. VII. 106; 9. IV. 313; 10. V. 128; 11. V. 142-43; 12. III. 193; 13. V. 375-76; 14. V. 25-26; 15. V. 19; 16. V. 8; 17. III. 173-74; 18. IV. 218; 19. V. 144-45; 20. III. 219; 21. III. 151; 22. III. 171; 23. V. 23; 24. II. 114; 25. VII. 145; 26. III. 270-71; 27. III. 172-73; 28. VII. 321; 29. III. 173; 30. III. 132; 31. V. 235; 32. I. 20; 33. VI. 332-33; 34. V. 138; 35. IV. 233; 36. I. 20; 37. V. 122; 38 VI. 294-95; 39. VI. 179; 40. VI. 355; 41. V. 13; 42. III. 212.

CHAPTER III

1. *Prabuddha Bharata*, January, 1947, 11; 2. *My Life and Mission*, 10; 3. IV. 157; 4. IV. 244; 5. IV. 385-91; 6. IV. 273-74; 7. VI. 224-25; 8. V. 7-9; 9. V. 2; 10. V. 12; 11. I. 145; 12. V. 270; 13. V. 21; 14. V. 2; 15. I. 427; 16. II. 113-14; 17. I. 422; 18. III. 245-46; 19. I. 428; 20. I. 429-34; 21. I. 387; 22. V. 143; 23. III. 296-97.

CHAPTER IV

1. III. 360-61; 2. III. 337-39; 3. V. 320; 4. III. 167; 5. III. 349-50; 6. V. 231; 7. V. 321-22; 8. V. 40; 9. VII. 300-3; 10. IV. 400; 11. V. 225-56; 12. III. 193-94; 13. V. 156; 14. VI. 285; 15. V. 96; 16. V. 194; 17. VII. 244-45; 18. III. 429; 19. V. 320-21; 20. VII. 418; 21. V. 23; 22. VI. 287-88.

CHAPTER V

1. V. 127; 2. IV. 317-18; 3. III. 294; 4. III. 298; 5. III. 291; 6. III. 291; 7. III. 297-98; 8. IV. 245-46; 9. VI. 80-81; 10. VI. 287; 11. III. 191-93; 12. VI. 386-87.

CHAPTER VI

1. IV. 385; 2. IV. 394; 3. IV. 397-403; 4. VI. 342-43; 5. V. 110; 6. V. 25; 7. VII. 146-47; 8. VII. 148; 9. V. 12-13; 10. V. 297; 11. VII. 308-10.